A DIFFERENT KIND OF HAPPINESS

May Your Joy Be Full

Tawana T. Thomas

Diligence Publishing Company
Bloomfield, New Jersey

The Scriptures in this book are from the King James Version and the New King James Version.

A DIFFERENT KIND OF HAPPINESS

Copyright © 2021 Tawana T. Thomas
c/o Diligence Publishing Company
P.O. Box 2476
Bloomfield, New Jersey

All Rights Reserved

No part of this book may be reproduced in any form without the written permission from the publisher except for brief passages included in a review.

To contact the author to preach or speak at your church, organization, seminar, or conference email:

A DIFFERENT KIND OF HAPPINESS

ISBN: 978-1-7374840-0-4

Printed in the United States

DEDICATION

This book is dedicated to all the
"Christian singles that desire to marry.
May your joy be full. May your mouth be filled
with laughter and your lips with rejoicing."

TABLE OF CONTENTS

DEDICATION 3
LOVE 7
INTRODUCTION 9
Chapter 1: Esteem, Love, and Belonging 11
Chapter 2: Family 15
Chapter 3: Coming Out of My Sisters' Shadow 17
Chapter 4: Matters of the Heart 21
Chapter 5: Relationships 25
Chapter 6: Loneliness 31
Chapter 7: Biblical Principles 35
Chapter 8: #Wife Material 39
Chapter 9: #Husband Material 43
Chapter 10: It Is All Up To Me 47
Chapter 11: The Promises of God 49
Chapter 12: Prayer 51
Chapter 13: Prayer 53
Epilogue 55
Appendix 57
MEET THE AUTHOR 59
ORDER INFORMATION 61

LOVE

1 Corinthians 13:4-8 (NKJV)

4. Love suffers long and is kind; love does not envy; love does not parade itself, is not puffed up.
5. does not behave rudely, does not seek its own, is not provoked, thinks no evil.
6. does not rejoice in iniquity, but rejoices in the truth;
7. bears all things, believes all things, hopes all things, endures all things.
8. Love never fails.

INTRODUCTION

Happiness is an emotional state of being that is difficult to explain because it is unique to us all. Happiness can be described as a state of being content or satisfied with oneself or one's circumstances. According to the Maslow' Hierarchy of Needs, this theory explains or helps define our humanistic need of motivation to obtain happiness.

The Five Levels of Maslow's Hierarchy of Needs are: physiological needs, safety needs, love and belonging needs, esteem needs, and self-actualization needs. Each level of Needs helps shape and develop the emotion or state of happiness.

God created us in a way that we all need socialization and communication; because as human beings, we are naturally relational beings.

Level One: **Physiological needs are food, water, warmth, and rest.**

Level Two: **Safety needs are personal security, resources, health, property, and employment.**

Level Three: **Love and belonging needs consist of friendship, intimacy, and a family sense of connection.**

Level Four: **Esteem needs consist of prestige, and a feeling of accomplishment.**

Level Five: **Self-Actualization is the desire to become the most that one can be.**

Which level of the Maslow Hierarchy of Needs do you identify with the most?

Now that you have identified your emotional state, what steps will you take to pursue happiness to accomplish your goals?

CHAPTER 1

Esteem, Love, and Belonging

The greatest teacher in life is the experiences that we gain from everyday challenges. One of the most valuable lessons that I have learned occurred during my time of employment as a Long-term substitute teacher. My assignment was to teach the music class for Public School Number 13, grades K-thru-8. Every day was a learning experience. Writing lesson plans was a learning experience. Gathering materials was a learning experience. Grading papers was a learning experience.

Captivating the student's attention was a learning experience. The lesson that engulfed us all was the class project based on Louis Armstrong's song "What a Wonderful World." According to the song's lyrics, the students had to draw or paint a picture of something that brought happiness to their lives.

A DIFFERENT KIND OF HAPPINESS

After listening to Louis Armstrong's "What a Wonderful World," some students began to feverishly write their ideas down. Some students shook their heads with the "I can do this" attitude.

Very few students questioned themselves because of the circumstances that they were dealing with.

One individual commented, "What if you don't have anything that makes you happy?"

I responded, "There has to be something that makes you laugh, that brings you a glimmer of hope, that brightens your day. For example, a flower growing out of the garden, or the sounds of birds chirping; there has to be something that you enjoy, that makes you happy... think about it."

Moving along according to the lesson plan timeline; the school atmosphere was filled with the excitement of expectation. Each student put their heart into their assignment. From the beginning to the end, from top to bottom, from left to right, the corridor walls of the school's basement were covered with the artwork of our students' beautiful artwork. The bright colors extended beyond the black frames.

Their eyes were lit with hope and appreciation because they identified the person, the place, or the thing that brought happiness into their lives.

What my students and I experienced was a Level Three need of Love and Belonging, and Level Four need of Esteem based on the Maslow Hierarchy of Needs.

This Level Three need of Love and Belonging allowed my students to identify the person, thing, or place that brought contentment or satisfaction within themselves; a connection of belonging to family, friends, or a pet helped each student to experience happiness.

Level Four-Needs provide esteem and a sense of accomplishment. The students produced their absolute best work with their art project because they had a chance to be creative and to express themselves in an uninhibited learning environment.

As an educator, I experienced Level-Five-Self-Actualization because I discovered something that I enjoyed doing; my purpose to enlighten, to empower, and to bring out the best in others. This makes me happy.

My students and I experienced a different kind of happiness. Despite our circumstances, we found a sense of love and belonging. Believe it or not, it is a wonderful world!

CHAPTER 2

Family

The marriage of Ivory and Gorothy Thomas provided me with ten siblings, and being a member of a large family never has a dull moment.

I am used to being in a house full of people. Holiday dinners, cooking on the grill, Dad's garden, and his fishing equipment are all fond memories. I think we were more excited about Daddy's fishing trips than he was – the fishing poles, the fishing line, the hooks, and the baits....

For one trip, he brought the bait home in a brown box; you know the kind that you would use to put donuts or pastry in. Well, needless to say, no donuts were in this box. Instead, some wiggly creatures covered in seaweed were. Someone came in the house late looking for something to eat, and, OH MY GOSH were they SURPRISED!!! A loud scream silenced the atmosphere as the rushed feet burst through the screen door. Everyone looked in shock and burst with laughter.

There was never a dull moment at the Thomas residence. Besides my mother, my father loved his children, especially his sons (his boys). His love for his children was reckless and unconditional. No matter what we did right or wrong, or wrong or right, Daddy was always there. He never stopped praying for us. He never stopped loving us.

When the grandchildren were born, there was a revival in his soul, and a different kind of happiness developed. It broke the silences of a quiet house. The silent giant smiled and laughed again.

CHAPTER 3

Coming Out of My Sisters' Shadow

Being the youngest sister of five girls has its advantages. They are always around to guide you and protect you. Growing up I always heard, "Oh, you are so and so sister, you're the baby girl!" which it is not a bad thing to be acknowledged as someone sibling. My sisters were active in the school community, school clubs, drill squads, fashion shows and music. Even in the church community of Monumental Baptist Church located on Lafayette Street in Jersey City, the Thomas family participated. Us girls participated.

Growing up with older sisters helped me to set a standard for myself. For example, I became selective about the kind of people that I would associate myself with, the kind of lifestyle that I would live, and yes, the kind of relationships that I chose to have.

Elder sisters are a guiding light. Each of my sisters taught me viable lessons that still guide me even today. For example:

- My eldest sister Genell spoiled me; she brought a sophistication to all our lives.
- Linda taught me how to fight, she would say with an adamant voice "Don't you let people tell you what you can and cannot do."
- Phyllis reminded me, "You always have to be a lady."
- Iris taught me how to be a go getter; not to wait for anyone.
- Melissa has always been my encourager, "Yeah Tawana, you can do it."
- Finally, my sister-in-law Zelda, who is very caring, knows how to smooth out the rough edges.

In addition, though not biologically related, through the years of friendship, these ladies have always been a great influence in my life: Beatrice, the fashion icon, Sheryl, the one that always checks on you to make sure you are all right, and Annette, the peace maker.

Coming out from my sisters' shadows I stand as a confident woman, a virtuous woman; no longer dictated by the world or religious standards, but rooted in the liberty and the love that the Lord Jesus Christ has provided for me. Knowing who I am brought me into a different kind of happiness, I am no longer living in my sisters' shadows.

CHAPTER 4

Matters of the Heart

I am not a miserable person, I love me. Society, or shall I say bullies, or shall I say insecure, or shall I say controlling individuals tend to label plus size women as being miserable, having low self- esteem, lazy, and so much more; which is the furthest thing from the truth.

The truth is there are plenty of voluptuous women, or shall I say, "Big Beautiful Women," that are virtuous women, filled with joy and peace, and have an active lifestyle. She is a true jewel.

"Lose a few pounds, and you will be alright!"

The first time this statement was spoken to me, I was a high school student.

During my high school years at Henry Snyder High School, I was highly active; I played girls basketball (Ms. Joyce was the coach) and tennis (Ms. Baletti, the science teacher was our tennis coach). I also participated in numerous clubs. The negative comment that the young man made about me "losing a few pounds" did not settle in my heart, but it lingered in the back of my mind.

My high school years were crucial because I had to be determined to not let the negative comments/the fat jokes dictate to me who I am and what I can and cannot do.

The greatest gift that I have given myself over the years was learning to love myself, to appreciate my uniqueness, flaws and all. Knowing how to love myself allowed me to develop into a woman who knows her worth. Referring to chapter 4 of my book "Healing of the Soul," and I quote, *"The Lord has taken the time to fashion you in his image. You are fearfully and wonderfully made."*

Throughout the days of my youth and adulthood I learned to look in the mirror and appreciate me, to love me, to speak life to me. I learned to use the negative comments about my weight as steppingstones. I have grown to be happy with me.

Strength and honor are her clothing;
and she shall rejoice in time to come.
Proverbs 31:25

CHAPTER 5

Relationships

Well, there will not be no tea spilling in this chapter, huh, huh... Anyways, a friend of mine said, "Tawana, now that your sons are older and establishing lives of their own, what about you?"

I remember thinking to myself, "Where is she going with this?"

She repeated herself about three times before I understood what she was hinting at... RELATIONSHIP!

Duh!

Over the years I have learned that relationships are complicated, but they are what you make them to be. At this stage in my life, I know what I want and what I will or will not tolerate. I had my fair share of heartaches. In response to her comment I stated, "I'm not going to open the door of my heart and home to any man just to keep from being alone."

I have been single all these years, and it is not going to hurt me to wait a bit longer. By God's grace I raised my sons, and I did my best to live a respectable lifestyle before them.

I read the books about singlehood, and I attended the women conferences and fellowships. I have been there and done that. Please Pastor(s), do not be offended if I do not attend another singles' meeting.

Speaking of books, a few years ago, I read Lurie Cole's book titled: *Beauty by The Book* (2007). The content on those pages illuminated the differences in the characteristics and behavior of women. They also served as a mirror which allowed me to see myself, flaws and all. It was a pivotal point when I decided which woman I chose to be, not allowing the labels placed by others to determine who I am. I chose to be a virtuous woman!

There is a distinction in behavior and character between a Christian and non-believer. As a Christian woman, my faith dictates my lifestyle, my fashion sense, and the way I treat or interact with people. My faith dictates the boundaries in my life. For example, it dictates what I will or will not do on a date night. If we are going to dinner, it will be just that; dinner, nothing more! We can be friends without benefits... You understand what I am saying. My advice to single women and men would be:

1. Not to lose your identity or your senses just to have a man or woman in your life. Do not dumb down to keep from being alone.

2. Know without a doubt that you deserve the best. Free yourself from toxic relationships.

3. Be realistic with your expectations; only God can meet your deepest needs.

One indicator that tells you if you are in a good and healthy relationship is, your life will improve for the better. He or she will bring out the best in you; they will compliment you. There is a certain kind of peace and order that he or she will bring into your life. Ladies, it is the nature of a man to pursue. Allow him to pursue you. Allow him to step in and be the man, the king in your life.

"Bishop R.C. Blakes Jr., the author of *Queenology,* gives great and sound advice for women from a male/father's perspective. I like the dating advice that he shares with women over forty. Ladies, the wisdom is pouring for the healing of the heart. The wisdom is pouring so that we can correct our behavior and think soberly regarding a potential male partner.

"A queen never connects herself to a man who does not model her values" (Blakes, 2017).

Connecting to a man that does not model your values is a recipe for destruction. Commonality is a major component in a relationship; being able to sit down and have a decent conversation is necessary in the development of a healthy relationship. Having the ability to understand each other's mood is a necessity for survival. Our culture, beliefs, and education play a major role in our social life, and who we acquaint ourselves with.

Why should I share my life with someone who does not value me as a person? The biggest mistake that you can ever make is trying to change someone for your liking. It is not a good idea to hang onto someone that wants something different in life. Wanting something different does not make him or her a bad person; it simply means your purpose and expectations are different, and it is okay to go your separate ways.

RELATIONSHIPS

Some years ago, I heard this analogy, "A peg box is made of different shapes, you cannot put a square in a star place, it will not fit; nor will a star fit in the space designed for the square every shape has its' proper place."

This truth applies to every individual that comes into our lives, with their own purpose or motives. Be careful and prayerful about your associations. Some individuals are genuinely good people. Some individuals are genuinely bad company.

CHAPTER 6

Loneliness

"Psychologists generally consider loneliness to be a stable trait, meaning that individuals have different set-points for feeling loneliness, and they fluctuate around these set-points depending on the circumstances in their lives" (Encyclopedia Britannica, 2018).

Sometimes being alone has a significant purpose. In some cases, being alone is not a bad thing, it gives you the time to become acquainted with yourself, to bring order in one's life, and to recommit yourself to the Lord Jesus Christ. Knowing that being alone is a temporary state, it gives us the opportunity to look at the whole picture and make the necessary improvements to better our lives.

I understand what psychologists are saying, because I experienced a sense of loneliness when my youngest son moved on campus. I repeatedly asked myself the same question, "What am I supposed to do now?" I must admit it; I found it difficult to adjust to the quietness in the house. It was difficult to think about how to reestablish a social life for myself.

One of my friend's mission is to introduce me to men that she thinks may be a good match for me. Another friend suggest that I try the dating websites. However, I prefer meeting face to face.

Another example of loneliness being a set trait in someone's life, is the silence that he or she is experiencing after the demise of a spouse. A co-worker of mine stated that "After family and friends go back home to their lives, the silence that accompanies being alone is something that I do not like."

I must agree, I do not like the silence either.

According to sociologist Robert S. Weiss, the father of the Attachment Theory, there are six social needs that must be met in order to not feel lonely. They are as follows: social integration, nurturance, reassurance of worth, sense of reliable alliance, and guidance in stressful situations. Weiss also emphasized that "Friendships complement, but do not substitute for a close, intimate relationship with a partner in staving off loneliness." (Loneliness, 2018)

This is why God, our Heavenly Father, the Creator of the universe stated, "It is not good for man to be alone" Genesis 2:18 (KJV).

God ordained marriage with a purpose in mind. Marriage is beneficial for both male and female, husband, and wife. Marriage reflects the union of God's relationship with the Church; marriage is a sacred union between man and woman.

Naturally, we are relational beings and there is nothing wrong with desiring friendship, companionship, and marriage. I earnestly believe if we are taught about the dynamics of relationships and marriages, we are better prepared intellectually and emotionally for relationships and for the commitment of marriage.

"Many waters cannot quench love, neither can the floods drown it."
Song of Solomon 8:7

CHAPTER 7

Biblical Principles

As Christian singles that choose to live by biblical principles, we do not want to put ourselves in harm's way or in a position of compromise, especially when courting or dating. We are admonished by the Apostle Paul in the book of 1 Corinthians chapter 6:9-20 and chapter 7 on the conduct of Christian singles. Verse 9 of chapter 6 states, "But if they cannot contain, let them marry: for it is better to marry than to burn."

I think a lot of couples use this scripture to justify a hasty decision to enter marriage blindly because they are looking at the physical benefits of marriage. However, if a couple were to take the time to look at the dynamics of marriage, knowing that men and women are equal, but their roles in marriage and home are different; they may proceed with marriage more prepared.

I believe that the Lord answers the prayers of His children, His servants. I believe He allows the paths of two individuals to cross; and during that moment of time, they will decide if they will pursue a relationship (get to know each other) or go their separate ways. A great biblical example of a divine connection can be found in the book of Genesis 24:1-67. Here we find that Abraham gave his eldest servant the task of finding a wife for his son Isaac. Abraham gave his eldest servant specific instructions on where to go to find a wife for Isaac. The eldest servant acknowledges the Lord as he traveled to Abraham's father's house. Listen to his prayer verses:

42 And I came this day unto the well, and said, **O Lord God of my master Abraham, if now thou do prosper my way which I go:**
43 **Behold, I stand by the well of water; and it shall come to pass, that when the virgin cometh forth to draw water, and I say to her, give me, I pray thee, a little water of thy pitcher to drink:**
44 **And she says to me, both drink thou and I will also draw for thy camels; let the same be the woman whom the Lord hath appointed out for my master's son.**

In verse 45, we see that the Lord answered the prayer of Abraham's servant "And before I had done speaking in mine heart**, behold** Rebekah **came forth**."

Ladies and gentlemen, for those that desire marriage, may the Lord prosper the way to your God ordained spouse.

CHAPTER 8

#Wife Material

I understand that every marriage is unique; you must come to an agreement to structure and build your lives together. From my understanding, learning to manage the incompatibilities will make a huge difference in one's marriage. From my understanding, marriage requires commitment and work; it will not be a bed of roses all the time, but every effort is worth it.

I asked my sister Melissa for some advice about marriage, and she stated:

*"Communication is important; you may not agree or see eye to eye, but you must respect your spouse's opinions or decisions, as well as they must respect your opinions and decisions."

*"**Never tell your girlfriend or friend everything about your marriage.**"

*"**Do not compare your marriage to someone else's.**"

The role of a wife is a prestigious role. She can nurture her husband's dreams, strengthen his hands, and she compliments him in every area. She is THE help mate. The wife cultivates her family. Home is first. Whether you are a stay-at-home mom or in the workforce, home is always first. She influences her workplace and community for the better.

In lieu of taking care of everyone else, she, the woman, the wife, must take care of herself as well. Taking care of oneself is more than a beauty treatment, nails done, and wearing nice clothes; mental health, physical health, and spiritual health is a priority. Because life requires much more than average, it is important for us women to be at our best: the best wife, the best mother, the best sister, the best auntie, the best you! Once again, we are not comparing ourselves to each other because every wife, every mother, every sister, every aunt, and every friend's role in life is unique.

Several years ago, I read *Beauty by the Book* written by Laurie Cole. The content on those pages helped me settle confidently within myself as a single woman of the Christian faith. The contents on those pages enlightened my understanding about the characteristics and behavior of women that can make or break a marriage. If you are anything like me, a big romantic, with a million questions racing in my mind; this book will answer some questions for you. She answered the questions I had in the chapter that spoke about the "Captivating Woman."

*"The Captivating woman elegantly, beautifully, and graciously accepts her husband." (Cole, 2017)

*"The power and passion of her love literally makes him real." (Cole, 2017)

You are a blessing, #a woman of integrity, # a woman of good character, # a woman of wisdom. The virtuous woman of Proverbs 31 has set the standard for many mothers and daughters. Thinking about my mother and how she raised her children, each of us had a special relationship

with her, yet she loved us all the same. My mother instilled in us the golden rule to live by, "God first, family second, everything else is last."

As a mother I had to learn how to balance my relationship with God, family, and everything else. God will never leave you. Your children are a blessing; their greatest purpose is to help you grow as an individual. We must learn to prioritize what is and who is important and be careful of who we allow in our lives.

One of the greatest modern models of a virtuous woman is Michelle Obama. Michelle Obama, a public figure who influenced girls and women from all walks of life, is intelligent, beautiful, strong, and poised. She is a virtuous woman. I believe the Lord has allowed our paths to cross with exemplary women that help perfect us in immeasurable ways.

Think about the virtuous women in your life. How did they influence you for the better?

Being the virtuous woman that you are, how can you influence the lives of other women, young ladies, and girls?

CHAPTER 9

#Husband Material

This is my perspective as to why God stated, "It is not good for man to be alone?"

1. Without man, humans will be extinct.
2. To keep man from perversion.
3. Man reflects the image of God Himself.

The purpose of man, the role of a husband, is vitally important. Being a husband is an honorable role in life. Do not believe the lie when a woman says, "I don't need a man."
We need you!
I found Ephesians Chapter 5, verses 20-30 interesting because it reflects Christ's relationship with the Church, and it provides the structure for marriage along with key details. I understand that we are all free-will creatures, yet despite our free will, we still need structure and order in marriage, and in our family. In

Ephesians 5:25, husbands are admonished to love their wives as Christ loved the church and gave Himself for it.

Reminiscing about my mother and father's marriage, their love story was the most beautiful novel that I have ever read. I am sure that they had their challenges, but we never witnessed any. My Father never disrespected my mother in the home nor in public. He was our dad, our dad only. He was the faithful husband of Gorothy Beatrice Thomas, no side chicks. We loved Valentine's day; Mom kept the gifts, and we ate the candies. One night, they surprised us by going out on a date. We were extremely excited to see Mommy and Daddy go out for an evening and enjoy themselves. They were so cute.

Husbands, you have to take the Mrs.' out for the evening. You need that time to reconnect and to enjoy each other privately. Do not let money be an issue. Be creative, or take advantage of discounts for couples. Do something to refresh your relationship!

Husbands, communication is a key factor to your relationship. Do not stop talking, and do not stop listening. She values your insight, your wisdom, and she values you.

Husbands, you are the priest of your home, you are the provider and the protector; as the husband you are not responsible for fulfilling the role of your wife's father.

The role of the priest is to cover his family spiritually in prayer and in devotion; with the purpose of leading your family to God by instilling values and morals into the children, teaching them true religion (James 1:27).

The role of the provider is to ensure that his family has shelter, food, clothing, and other necessities to make life suitable, per your taste. We all like nice things and there is nothing wrong with having nice things, living in nice communities, and driving nice cars. There is more to life than paying bills. We all must be realistic. We all must live within our means. Manage your finances, save, pay off debt. Your greatest asset is your family (Psalm 127).

The role of the protector is to do just that, protect! Protect your wife and protect your family by providing a safe place for you and yours and not putting yourself or them in harm's way. Just like Christ protected and defended the Church, the husband is to do the same for his wife and family.

I know that this is common knowledge but sometimes our sons and our men need to be encouraged to know that they have what it takes to be a good husband and to be a good father.

Marriage is a covenant relationship between man and woman in the presence of God. Marriage is a good thing, it is beneficial psychologically, physically, and financially. Marriage is a good thing.

CHAPTER 10

It Is All Up to Me

I love the scripture, "God has given us the power to get wealth." Deuteronomy 8:18 (KJV)

God has given us the ability to accrue, to gain, to produce happiness, joy, peace, and love; and He has given us the ability to live the life of our dreams or desires. We do not have to compromise; we do not have to cheat or steal to get it or settle for less. "God has given us the power to get wealth."

In this case, the decisions that we make will bring forth contentment and satisfaction to our lives. Let me ask, the relationships that we are involved in, do we eliminate some, in order to not allow people to live vicariously through us? Or do we salvage others; nurture and build those relationships that help us to grow and add value to our lives?

Yes, sometimes the choices of life may seem complicated, but responding through wisdom, we can choose what is best and who is best for us.

Surprisingly in Proverbs 3:13 it states, "Happy is the man that findeth wisdom, and the man that getteth understanding." (KJV)

Never feel bad about the choices that you prayed and fasted about. There will be some individuals that will make great efforts to discourage or attempt to prove you wrong. I am convinced that you must believe in your prayers, and you must follow the leading of God's Holy Spirit. You must trust God in every area of your life.

Trust Him to bring you into your wealthy place of joy, peace, love, hope, and laughter. You must trust God to cultivate you into a delightsome land; where you are no longer barren, but fruitful in relationship with a significant other. Everyone needs love. Everyone needs a friend. At this stage in my life, I am no longer allowing fear to dictate if I am ready or willing to love again. Through Christ Jesus, I have a different kind of happiness!

CHAPTER 11

The Promises of God

The greatest love that I ever experienced in life came through my encounter with my Lord and Savior Jesus Christ. The love of God is unconditional. I do not have to jump through hoops to prove myself or earn it, His love has always been available and accessible. The love of God helped me to embrace my single state, the love of God helped me to overcome loneliness; and take comfort in the Word of God.

*I have loved thee with an everlasting love therefore with lovingkindness have I drawn thee. (Jeremiah 31:3)

*I will never leave thee nor forsake thee. (Hebrews 13:5)

*He will not fail thee, nor forsake thee. (Deuteronomy 31:16)

*My beloved spoke and said unto me, Rise up, my love, my fair one and come away. (Song of Solomon 2:10)

*Till he fills thy mouth with laughing and thy lips with rejoicing. (Job 8:21)

*Behold, I have graven thee upon the palms of my hands: the walls are continually before me. (Isaiah 49:16)

*Keep me as the apple of the eye, hide me under the shadow of thy wings. (Psalm 17:8)

*For I am persuaded, that neither death, nor life, nor angels, nor principalities, nor powers, nor things present, nor things to come. (Romans 8:38) Nor height, nor depth, nor any other creature, shall be able to separate us from the love of God, which is in Christ Jesus our Lord. (Romans 8:39)

CHAPTER 12

Prayer

Thank You Father God, for filling my mouth with laughter and my lips with praise. As I draw from You the wells of salvation, thank You for beautifying my life with joy, peace, love, and happiness.

I thank You Father God for loving me with an everlasting love; I am grateful for Your kindness. I thank You Father God for never leaving me, nor forsaking me. Thank You for Your faithfulness.

I thank You Father God for never failing me, I trust You Lord God because You are not like man; You are consistent with me. Thank You for mending my heart, for healing my soul. Thank You, Father God, for blessing me with a different kind of happiness. Thank You.

In Your Matchless Name Lord Jesus Christ, I pray. AMEN, AMEN, AMEN.

CHAPTER 13

Prayer

Father God, I thank You for Your Holy Spirit resting upon me. I thank You for the anointing to preach good tidings unto the meek. I thank You for the anointing to set the captives free. Therefore, in Your Mighty Name of the Lord Jesus Christ, Jehovah Rapha; I speak healing to the brokenhearted, be mended in Jesus' name. I speak liberty to those imprisoned by rejection, abandonment, and oppression; be free in the Name of Jesus Christ. Beloved I wish above all things that you will prosper and be in good health as your soul prospers. Beloved I wish above all things that your most holy faith is strengthened. May the Lord grant you the desires of your heart as you delight yourself in Him. Father God we take confidence in Your Word that You will not withhold any good thing from Your children because You have given us life and life more abundantly. I thank You Father God for doing a new thing in me, for perfecting me. I thank You Father God for filling me and baptizing me in the fire of Your Holy Spirit.

In the Mighty name of Jesus Christ, I pray. AMEN, AMEN, AMEN.

Epilogue

I am sorry that you gave up on love and marriage; you have a right to feel that way.

I choose to believe in the power of love. That husband that the Lord gave you is a blessing, that wife that the Lord gave you is a blessing.

Yes, I am a big romantic at heart. I believe marriage is a beautiful thing. What makes marriage so grand is that you can share your life with someone that you love. It is about maturing, growing, and it is about fulfillment, joy, peace, and working through the challenges of life.

I encourage you not to rush the process, but learn about the dynamics of relationships and marriage. Use that knowledge to make the right choice for you. Use that knowledge to break the cycle of toxic relationships and establish healthy relationships. Honor your marriage vows. Honor each other.

Marriage is about a Different Kind of Happiness.

Appendix

The Agapekind Media, WAR for Marriage Restoration (Day 1): Call Forth Your Marriage - YouTube, Feb 2018.

BLAKES Jr. RC, QUEENOLOGY, 2017, Untapped Potential Publishing, rcblakes.com

BLAKES RC, Never Continue With a Man That Shames You, https://youtube/mvMm-PHM0MA, https://youtube.com/c/RobertBlakes,

Cherry Kendra, reviewed by Rachel Goldman, PhD, FTOS, What is Happiness, updated on October 22, 2020, www.Verywellmind.com

Cole Laurie, Beauty by The Book, 2007, 2017, Page 87,
www.priorityministries.org

Gungor Mark, DR, Laugh Your Way to a Better Marriage, 2008, Atria Paperback, www.markgungor.com

Hawkley, L. (2018, December 6). Loneliness. Encyclopedia Britannica. https://www.britannica.com/science/loneliness

Jakes T.D, nothing just happens, Feb 9, 2014, retrieved from T.D. Jakes Sermons: Nothing Just Happens - YouTube, tdjakes.org

Biblical Reference: retrieved from King James Version The Holy Bible, Holman Bible Publishers, Nashville, Tennessee

C: 1 Corinthians 6:9-20

D: Deuteronomy 18:18, 31:16, 31:25

G: Genesis 2:18, Genesis 24:1-67

H: Hebrews 13:15

I: Isaiah 49:16

J: Jeremiah 31:3, Job 8:21

P: Proverbs 3:13, Proverbs 31:25, Psalms 139:17, Psalms 17:8

R: Romans 8:38, Romans 8:39

S: Song of Solomon 2:10, 8:7

MEET THE AUTHOR

Tawana Thomas has been chosen for such a time as this. She has a spirit of boldness and a willingness to fight the good fight of faith without fear. This represents the foundation of who she is in Christ. She is fondly called the W.W.E. Diva of the Kingdom of God. She is willing to wrestle until a breakthrough emerges. She will not give up on her assignment until God blesses her, and she teaches other women that they have the same power and anointing as well.

Miss Thomas believes serving begins at home. She is actively involved with the Christian Education Department and the Missions Department at church because the Lord has instilled in her heart the mandate to feed His sheep. He has divinely connected her with individuals who have encouraged, supported, prayed, and worked with her so that she is equipped to pay it forward.

A single parent of two wonderful, handsome boys; she recognizes they are incredibly supportive of her endeavors. She began her career in the financial industry, but spends her time today as a certified public speaker and an educator.

She is the founder of Power Point International Ministry and the Iconic Agency.

Tawana T. Thomas is a woman of substance living with the purpose to empower, encourage and liberate the lives of others through the Word of God.

For booking or general inquiries email: t8Wana16@gmail.com

ORDER INFORMATION

You can order additional copies of *A Different Kind of Happiness* by emailing the author directly using the email address below.

Tawana T. Thomas

Email Address: t8Wana16@gmail.com

Books are available at Amazon.com, BN.com Kindle and Your Local Bookstores (By Request)

Please leave a review for this book on Amazon and let other readers know how much you enjoyed reading it.

Thank you!